Endorsements for the Church Questions Series

"Christians are pressed by very real questions. How does Scripture structure a church, order worship, organize ministry, and define biblical leadership? Those are just examples of the questions that are answered clearly, carefully, and winsomely in this new series from 9Marks. I am so thankful for this ministry and for its incredibly healthy and hopeful influence in so many faithful churches. I eagerly commend this series."

R. Albert Mohler Jr., President, The Southern Baptist Theological Seminary

"Sincere questions deserve thoughtful answers. If you're not sure where to start in answering these questions, let this series serve as a diving board into the pool. These minibooks are winsomely to-the-point and great to read together with one friend or one hundred friends."

Gloria Furman, author, *Missional Motherhood* and *The Pastor's Wife*

T0327141

"As a pastor, I get asked lots of questions. I'm approached by unbelievers seeking to understand the gospel, new believers unsure about next steps, and maturing believers wanting help answering questions from their Christian family, friends, neighbors, or coworkers. It's in these moments that I wish I had a book to give them that was brief, answered their questions, and pointed them in the right direction for further study. Church Questions is a series that provides just that. Each booklet tackles one question in a biblical, brief, and practical manner. The series may be called Church Questions, but it could be called 'Church Answers.' I intend to pick these up by the dozens and give them away regularly. You should too."

Juan R. Sanchez, Senior Pastor, High Pointe Baptist Church, Austin, Texas

"Where can we Christians find reliable answers to our common questions about life together at church—without having to plow through long, expensive books? The Church Questions booklets meet our need with answers that are biblical, thoughtful, and practical. For pastors, this series will prove a trustworthy resource for guiding church members toward deeper wisdom and stronger unity."

Ray Ortlund, President, Renewal Ministries

How Do I Fight Sin and Temptation?

Church Questions

How Do I
Fight Sin and
Temptation?

J. Garrett Kell

CROSSWAY®

WHEATON, ILLINOIS

Library of Congress Cataloging-in-Publication Data

Names: Kell, J. Garrett, author.
Title: How do I fight sin and temptation? / J. Garrett Kell.
Description: Wheaton, Illinois : Crossway, 2024. | Series: Church questions | Includes bibliographical references and index.
Identifiers: LCCN 2023019716 (print) | LCCN 2023019717 (ebook) | ISBN 9781433591785 (trade paperback) | ISBN 9781433591792 (pdf) | ISBN 9781433591808 (epub)
Subjects: LCSH: Sin—Biblical teaching. | Temptation—Biblical teaching. | Sin—Christianity.
Classification: LCC BT715 .K35 2024 (print) | LCC BT715 (ebook) | DDC 241/.3—dc23/eng/20230821
LC record available at https://lccn.loc.gov/2023019716
LC ebook record available at https://lccn.loc.gov/2023019717

Crossway is a publishing ministry of Good News Publishers.

BP		33	32	31	30	29	28	27	26	25	24
15	14	13	12	11	10	9	8	7	6	5	4	3	2	1

No temptation has overtaken you that is not common to man. God is faithful, and he will not let you be tempted beyond your ability, but with the temptation he will also provide the way of escape, that you may be able to endure it.

1 Corinthians 10:13

Greg was a gangster whose life was marked by nearly every evil imaginable. But God mercifully intervened and sent someone to share the gospel with him. After months of wrestling with what it means to follow Jesus, he surrendered to God, was baptized, and began his new life in Christ. He had been born again.

But giving his life to Jesus didn't make everything easier. Some parts of his life became harder.

When Greg was born again, it was as if he woke up in a world he didn't recognize. He had new feelings, strange convictions, and lingering concerns about whether he was making good choices.

What Greg didn't understand was that he was on the front lines of a spiritual war. He was forgiven and loved by God, but now he had a prowling adversary who lurked in the shadows, scheming to destroy him (John 10:10; 2 Cor. 2:11; 1 Pet. 5:8). To follow Jesus over the long haul, Greg needed to learn how to fight sin and temptation.

This book is for people like Greg. It seeks to explain what sin and temptation are and how to combat them with God's grace. These pages serve as an introduction to this lifelong pursuit, and I pray God will help you apply these lessons faithfully.

The Good Life

Humanity's first home was a garden of delight. God designed it with brilliant colors, sweet smells, and delicious fruits. He created our first parents, Adam and Eve, with the capacity to enjoy the garden's pleasures and, even more, to enjoy him.

This life with God was "very good" (Gen. 1:31). There was no shame or sorrow. No regrets or guilt. No depression or death. Life was perfect. But enjoying this abundant life depended on one thing: obedience to God's command. God invited them to "freely eat" of every tree in the garden except for one (Gen. 2:16 NASB).

But rather than obey God, they succumbed to temptation and sinned against him. Their rebellion not only brought death but also robbed them of all the good things God had for them. God cursed them and sent them out of the garden and away from his presence.

Today, we live in a world that abounds with evil. We live outside the garden and, like Greg, face an adversary who schemes to ensnare us in sin. Sin grieves God, harms others, and destroys our lives. Sounds scary, huh? Thankfully, we don't have to navigate this minefield alone. Jesus came to save us from sin's penalty, deliver us from sin's power, and enable us to resist sin's corrupting presence. In Christ, we have grace to oppose Satan's attacks and walk in the abundant life.

If we want to resist sin and enjoy the good life God has for us in Christ, then we need to first talk about what sin is.

What Is Sin?

One catechism defines sin this way: "What is sin? Sin is rejecting or ignoring God in the world he created, not being or doing what he requires in his law."[1] Or as artist Shai Linne says, "What is sin? Sin is the breaking of God's law plus our condition, which means from birth we all got flaws."[2]

Sin is in us and comes out of us. We are born with a sin nature, and even after we become Christians, we still battle with ongoing sin. Sin appears in our affections and our actions, in what we desire and what we do, in what we seek and what we say. It consists in doing what we shouldn't (sins of commission) and in not doing things we should (sins of omission).

Sin Is Personal (Ps. 51:4)

Sin is also personal. During the Last Supper, Peter assured Jesus that he would die for him

(Luke 22:33). Jesus, however, knew that Peter would succumb to temptation and deny him three times. Over the next few hours, Peter did just that. While Jesus was being beaten and wrongly accused, Peter distanced himself from his master, and even said "I do not know him" (Luke 22:57). As soon as the rooster crowed, "the Lord turned and looked at Peter," causing Peter to recognize his sin against a man he loved and had followed for three years (Luke 22:61). We then read that Peter "went out and wept bitterly" (Matt. 26:75; Luke 22:62).

In other words, sin doesn't merely break an arbitrary rule. It rejects God, who is personal. It effectively says to him, "I do not love you. I will not follow you. I will not obey you" (see Ps. 78:40; Isa. 43:24; Eph. 4:30). When Jesus looked into Peter's eyes, he suddenly felt the weight of his betrayal. He had denied the one who had only ever loved him.

Or think of that famous story about King David committing adultery with the wife of one of his soldiers and then arranging the man's murder. The Lord sent the prophet Nathan to expose David (2 Sam.12), and David's subsequent prayer shows how personal sin is. He cries out to God, "Against you, you only, have I sinned and done what is evil in your sight" (Ps. 51:4). Sin is always against God, and it's always personal.

Sin Is Painful (Prov. 22:5)

It's also painful. God designed life in this world to be lived in line with his law. This means that the world is "rigged"—rigged to work best by obeying God. Sinning, however, brings painful consequences. In Jesus's story of the prodigal son, for instance, a younger brother spends all his wealth on prostitutes, parties, and perversion. Maybe he has fun in the beginning, but soon enough the consequences catch up with him, and he finds himself sharing slop with swine (Luke 15:11–32).

I'm not saying that obedience always brings happiness and sin sadness. Yet the Bible teaches again and again that "the way of transgressors is hard" (Prov. 13:15 KJV) and "thorns and snares are in the way of the crooked" (Prov. 22:5). As a pastor, I've sat with hundreds of people who compromised with sin and suffered the consequences. As a believer who struggles with my own sin, I've compromised countless times to my shame. Sin promises to be sweet, but its aftertaste is always bitter.

Sin Is Punishable (Rom. 6:23)

Sin is also punishable. My family was driving down a country road recently when one of my children exclaimed, "That's a lot of tombstones!" As I looked, I saw an entire hillside lined with gravesites.

The picture of all the graves reminded me of God's warning that sin would bring death. God had said to Adam, "In the day that you eat of [the forbidden tree] you shall surely die" (Gen. 2:17). Or as Paul later explained, "The wages of sin is death" (Rom. 6:23).

But physical death is merely the "first death." The second death is far worse. The book of

Revelation contains a harrowing vision of the day of judgment, harrowing at least for those who do not know Jesus:

> Then I saw a great white throne and him who was seated on it. From his presence earth and sky fled away, and no place was found for them. And I saw the dead, great and small, standing before the throne, and books were opened. Then another book was opened, which is the book of life. And the dead were judged by what was written in the books, according to what they had done.... Then Death and Hades were thrown into the lake of fire. This is the second death, the lake of fire. And if anyone's name was not found written in the book of life, he was thrown into the lake of fire. (Rev. 20:11–15)

Sinning against God has great consequences. It separates us from relationship with him and incites his righteous, eternal wrath (Isa. 59:2; 2 Thess. 1:7–9).

Sin Is Pardonable (Isa. 55:7)

Gratefully, sin remains pardonable. Though our sin is great, God's grace is greater (Rom. 5:20). Punishment is his "strange" work (Isa. 28:21). He doesn't want to punish. He desires none to perish but for all to "turn, and live" (Ezek. 18:32; cf. 1 Tim. 2:4). God cried out through the prophet Isaiah,

> Let the wicked forsake his way, . . .
> let him return to the LORD, that He may
>   have compassion on him,
> . . . for he will abundantly pardon.
>   (Isa. 55:7)

In pursuit of this pardon, God loved the world and sent his Son to die for our sins and then rise again so that we could be forgiven (John 3:16). The good news offered to us is that God will not only forgive us if we turn to Christ but also empower us to fight sin (Titus 2:12–13). This means that, if we are trusting in Christ, we don't have to be dominated by sin any longer. We can walk in freedom and joy (Gal. 5:16–17).

What Is Temptation?

In addition to understanding sin, we also need to understand temptation and how it relates to our sin. Maybe a few stories will help:

Sarah sighed as she glanced at her phone. It was another message from her coworker Brian. He was charming, funny, and dangerous—at least to her. She knew a date with him was off-limits because he showed little interest in Christianity. At the same time, she was tired of being overlooked by the single men at church. Brian, on the other hand, flirted with her and flattered her. This awakened something inside her that she enjoyed and wanted to pursue. But she knew she shouldn't.

With situations like this in mind, the apostle James vividly describes how sin and temptation work: "Each person is tempted when he is lured and enticed by his own desire. Then desire when it has conceived gives birth to sin, and sin when it is fully grown brings forth death" (James 1:14–15).

Sin acts as an angler who baits the hook with a deceptive lure. The lure then floats along in front of us, and our sinful flesh is enticed. We crave what God forbids and give ourselves convincing reasons to succumb: "One look won't hurt." "You'll miss out if you don't." "It's not a big deal." "God will forgive you." "Just this one time." "You deserve this."

If we surrender to our evil desires instead of God's Spirit, then sin comes to fruition. Sin rewards us with an initial rush of enjoyment and sense of satisfaction. But that sense of fulfillment is eventually replaced with regret, which affords an opportunity for repentance. But if we resist repentance, sin's influence in us grows like a cancerous tumor in the soul, and we can become calloused to God. Inevitably, death results.[3]

Temptation, therefore, is not a friendly voice but a deadly invitation. To better understand the nature of temptation, let's consider what it isn't and what it is.

Temptation Is Not Iniquity (Matt. 4:1–11)

Reid was plagued by anger. In heated moments, he had an impulse to punch tables—or worse, people. His background as a brawler was difficult to escape. But just because he was tempted with outbursts of anger didn't mean he was sinning.

Scripture repeatedly warns us not to give in to temptation. For instance, God warned Cain, "Sin is crouching at the door. Its desire is contrary to you, but you must rule over it" (Gen. 4:7). Likewise, Paul told the Ephesian church what my friend Reid needed to regularly hear: "Be angry and do not sin" (Eph. 4:26).

Scripture repeatedly shows us that temptation and sin are not the same. Jesus was tempted by Satan yet escaped without sinning (Matt. 4:1–11; Heb. 4:15). By the power of the Spirit, we too can resist temptation (Rom. 6:1–14; 1 Cor. 10:13). Jesus taught us to pray "lead us not into temptation" because he is eager to help us resist it (Matt. 6:13).

Feeling anger doesn't necessitate being bitter, cursing, punching, or murdering. Being tempted with wrongful attraction doesn't need to lead to lust, masturbation, or adultery. Considering sin doesn't have to mean conceding to it. Knowing this keeps you from being crippled by unnecessary guilt; it gives hope to keep fighting, even when temptation is raging. It is possible, by the power of the Spirit, to be tempted by sin and not give in (Rom. 6).[4]

Temptation Is Not Immaturity (Phil. 3:12)

Daniel's battle with anxiety hadn't improved much over the years. He still hated flying; his palms still sweat before walking into a crowded room. He still struggled to sleep because his mind often raced with anxious thoughts. Yet he had been intentionally fighting sinful anxiety for years. At times, he wondered if he'd matured at all.

But abiding temptation is not always evidence of immaturity. Just because temptation continually haunts believers doesn't mean they aren't becoming more like Jesus. Until we see Jesus, we will continue to suffer temptation. So don't be discouraged just because temptation won't stop calling.

Temptation Is Not Irresistible (1 Cor. 10:13)

At times, temptation seems impossible to resist. Gossip felt this way for Shannon. Being in
the know empowered her. Seeking and sharing
information about others made her feel important and included. She knew being exalted at
other people's expense was wrong, but it was
the only way she knew how to connect with
her friends.

Temptation sometimes feels irresistible. God
assures us it is not. "God is faithful, and he will
not let you be tempted beyond your ability"
(1 Cor. 10:13). The Holy Spirit promises power
for self-control. He enables us to speak edify-
ing words instead of destructive words (Eph.
4:29–30). Believe this: the same power that
raised Jesus from the dead enables us believers
to resist any temptation we face.

Temptation Is an Invitation from Satan (Gen. 3:1–5)

Genesis 3 records the fall of humanity into sin.
Genesis tells us that Satan slithered up to Eve

in the garden of Eden with one thing in mind: to convince her to forsake her God. His sinister whisper worked: "Did God actually say?" (Gen. 3:1). His invitation to know "good and evil" in a way that was "like God" seemed liberating (Gen 3:5). He led her thoughts away from a "sincere and pure devotion" to God (2 Cor. 11:3). Through temptation, Satan invites us to sin against God while promising happiness apart from God. He calls us to forsake God's provision for a fleeting pleasure. He entices us to sin and falsely assures us, like he did Eve, that "you will not surely die" (Gen. 3:4). Meanwhile God truthfully assures us that sin "wage[s] war against your soul" (1 Pet. 2:11).

Understanding the nature of temptation should sober us. It reminds us that no matter how good temptation makes sin appear, it's a mirage. The temptation to be stingy is an invitation from Satan to resist the generosity that reflects Jesus. The impulse to click on pornography is an invitation from Satan to grieve God for a quick rush of lust. The urge to hurry your prayers and neglect Bible reading is an invitation to trust your wisdom over God's. Temptation stokes pride and tells you that you deserve to be at the center of the universe. Indulging in its fleeting offerings only leaves us empty and full of regret.

God, however, has a better way. His path leads to life (Matt. 7:13–14). Everything he promises comes true (Num. 23:19; Heb. 10:23). Everything he gives is good (Luke 11:10–13). His invitation is to a life of abundance now and forevermore (John 10:10; Rev. 21–22). Let us all forsake Satan's call and fight to follow God by faith.

Why Must I Fight?

If we stoke the fires of faith with Scripture-saturated motivation, we will be better positioned to produce God-pleasing obedience. Before we consider *how* to fight sin, let us consider *why* we fight it.

Fight for Your Salvation

First, fight for your salvation. That doesn't mean we fight to *earn* our salvation. Jesus did that for us. He lived perfectly, died suffi-ciently, and rose victoriously in our place. We are given a right standing with God by grace alone through faith alone in the finished work of Christ alone.

At the same time, the Bible teaches that true faith shows itself with Christlike works (James 2:14–26). For this reason, Scripture exhorts us, "Strive . . . for the holiness without which no one will see the Lord" (Heb. 12:14). It warns us: "the unrighteous will not inherit the kingdom of God" (1 Cor. 6:9; cf. Eph. 5:5). God rewards those who persevere in faith with the inheri-tance of salvation (Matt. 24:13).

Therefore, fight for your salvation. Don't harden your heart against God's word or grieve his Spirit, but rather, as Scripture ex-horts, "lay aside every weight, and sin which clings so closely, and let us run with endur-ance the race that is set before us, looking to Jesus, the founder and perfecter of our faith" (Heb. 12:1–2). Fight sin so that you will not shrink from him in shame at his coming (1 John 2:28).

Fight for Your Joy

Second, we should fight for the sake of joy. Jesus told his disciples that obeying his commands was essential to experiencing his joy: "These things I have spoken to you, that my joy may be in you, and that your joy may be full" (John 15:11). Resisting sin is how we partake of true joy. The joy of Jesus comes with no regrets. It's pure and life-giving.

Sadly, we too often exchange eternal pleasures for fleeting ones. When we sin, we settle for lesser joys. C. S. Lewis captured this tragedy beautifully:

> If we consider the unblushing promises of reward, and the staggering nature of the rewards promised in the Gospels, it would seem that our Lord finds our desires not too strong, but too weak. We are half-hearted creatures, fooling about with drink and sex and ambition, when infinite joy is offered us, like an ignorant child who wants to go on making mud pies in the slum when he cannot imagine what is meant by the offer

of a holiday at the sea. We are far too eas-
ily pleased.[5]

Jesus doesn't want you to settle for the cheap
thrills of sin. He wants to transform your desires so that you will love true joy instead of
counterfeit joys.

Fight for God's Pleasure

Next, we should fight for the sake of pleasing
God. In fact, our primary motivation for fighting
sin is love for God. We "keep his commandments
and do what pleases him" because we love him
(1 John 3:22). I mentioned earlier that sin is always personal—we sin against a personal God.
Well, the flipside is also true. Obedience is personal as well. Think about this: our every thought,
word, and action is done before the watching eyes
of God (Prov. 5:21). Rather than sin and grieve
God, "we make it our aim to please him" (2 Cor.
5:9; cf. Eph. 4:30). Obeying him is not burden-
some because we *love him* (1 John 5:3)!

Our obedience before God is personal.
As Paul says, we must "try to discern what is

pleasing to the Lord" (Eph. 5:10). We search the Scriptures to discover what brings him delight and then set our hearts to do it (Ps. 119:11, 18–19; Col. 1:10). We sacrifice to serve others, knowing "such sacrifices are *pleasing to God*" (Heb. 13:16). Even if we do sin, we can please him by confessing it because "we speak, not to please man, but to please God who tests our hearts" (1 Thess. 2:4; Gal. 1:10; 1 John 2:1–2).

Struggling believer, plead with God to give you both the desire and the strength to obey him. He promises he will answer (Phil. 2:13). Surround yourself with godly friends who inspire you to avoid what grieves God and grow in what pleases him (1 Thess. 4:1). He is pleased when his people approach him in faith and trust that he will answer (Heb. 11:6).

How *Not* to Fight Sin

Fighting sin is spiritual warfare, and warfare requires a battle plan. If left to our own devices, we would have little success against our unseen enemy. Thankfully, God's word supplies wisdom to assist us in eluding the evil one's snares. We'll begin by briefly considering how not to engage in the battle, followed by practical tactics to flee sin and follow God.

Don't Fight Sin by Ignoring It

Pretending sin isn't there won't help you fight it, as with Ben. Ben was a jokester, but at times his jesting became inappropriate. He turned innocent comments into crude remarks and occasionally used off-color language to get a laugh. When conviction came, he rationalized it away. He'd think, "I didn't really mean it. It's not who I really am. It's not that big of a deal. I'm free in Christ."

An unwillingness to admit sin prevents you from repenting of it.

Don't Fight Sin by Entertaining It

We also can't fight by entertaining sin, as with Jess. Jess struggled with body image. She envied girls who *seemed* to lose weight effortlessly and looked beautiful in whatever they wore. Her insecurity tempted her to envy others, hate herself, and have an unhealthy relationship with food. She noticed that spending time on certain social media apps made things worse. Yet rather than deleting those apps, she allowed herself to linger, fantasizing about the life she'd have if she were thinner. She wanted to test her resolve and prove that she was strong enough to live a "normal" life.

The problem, however, is that entertaining temptation enables sin. Our flesh grows stronger and our resolve weaker with every lingering dose. You can't manage sin; you must kill it.

Don't Fight Sin by Indulging It

Sin wants us to think that if we will indulge in it, it will be satisfied and go away. The fact is, feeding our sin only strengthens it.

We see this principle play out in one of the most horrific stories in the Bible. Second Samuel 13 tells us the tragic story of Amnon, one of the sons of King David. Amnon had a lustful obsession with Tamar. He fanaticized about being with her to the point that he tricked her into a compromising situation and raped her. His "love" for her quickly turned to hatred (2 Sam. 13:15). Indulging his sinful impulses only inflamed more sin; it didn't extinguish his wrong desires. Do not be deceived: giving sin what it wants only empowers it to want more.

Don't Fight Sin by Exchanging It

A shallow fight with sin will settle for substituting one sin for another. Jim's impulsive spending was destroying his life. So he took great measures to halt his poor stewardship. He set a budget, got accountability, and even froze his credit cards. The problem, however, is that Adam began to indulge in excessive eating. Like an uncured disease with a new symptom, his impulsive lack of self-control merely manifested itself in another area.

Don't just exchange one sin for another; aim to eliminate it and replace it with a greater affection for Christ.[6]

How to Fight Sin and Temptation

If those are the ways *not* to fight, how *should* we fight sin and temptation?

Call Out for God's Help (Matt. 6:13)

When Jesus taught his disciples to pray, he included a striking instruction: Pray for protection against temptation. Hear his words afresh, "Lead us not into temptation, but deliver us from evil" (Matt. 6:13).[7] Jesus not only taught his disciples to pray this way but also embodied it. When he faced his greatest temptation in the garden of Gethsemane, he twice exhorted them "Pray that you may not enter into temptation" (Luke 22:40, 46).

Our single greatest weapon against sin and temptation is prayer. Prayer is an admission of humble dependence on God. It lifts our eyes away from sin and places them on Jesus. Through prayer, we "resist the devil" and "draw near to God" (James 4:7–8). Through it, we confess our desire to sin and plead for help to resist it. When you are tempted, pray to God. He is the

one who helps us and will keep us from falling
(Ps. 121:3).

1. Pray before Temptation

Just as armies prepare before going into battle, so
we must pray before a spiritual battle. Ask God
each morning, during the day, and before bed to
protect you from temptation. If you know you're
entering a unique season of vulnerability to sin,
entreat others to join you in prayer.

2. Pray during Temptation

If you were stranded on a raft in the ocean
and saw a boat in the distance, you would fire
off a flare to signal for help. In the same way,
when temptation approaches, fire up the flare
of prayer. The Scriptures are filled with brief,
helpful prayers that you can model your own
cry for help after:

> "Save us, Lord; we are perishing." (Matt.
> 8:25)

> "Lord, save me." (Matt. 14:30)

"Lord, help me." (Matt. 15:25)

"Lord, have mercy on us." (Matt. 20:30, 31)

"I believe; help my unbelief." (Mark 9:24)

Recently, I was bombarded with angry selfishness. So, I went to my room, closed the door, knelt down, and prayed something like this: "God, I confess I'm overwhelmed. I want what I want in this situation, and I'm irritable and grumpy and short-tempered. I feel unappreciated, and it's tempting me to be mean. Help me speak tenderly. Help me imitate Jesus." I battled with my flesh for several minutes until God mercifully granted me peace to emerge from my room with fresh strength to love others.

3. Pray after Temptation

If you faced an opportunity to sin and resisted, thank God for it. Remember that he is the one who gives us grace for every good work. Learning to cultivate a heart of thankfulness not only honors God but also fuels further obedience.

If you give in to temptation, remember to turn back to the grace of God found in Jesus Christ. Repent of your sin, reject it, and confess to God your sin and what promises of his you failed to believe. Ask God to give you the strength to reject that sin in the future and start walking in holiness afresh.

4. Pray with Others

We are too weak to fight sin by ourselves. Enlist good friends to pray with you and for you. Share with them when you are feeling tempted and ask them to join you in seeking the Lord's protection. Don't grow discouraged if they don't check in on you, just keep reaching out, update them on how the battle is going, and keep asking for help.

The apostle James assures us that "[we] do not have because [we] do not ask"—including protection from temptation (James 4:2). Some of us endure unrelenting temptation because we have not asked God to protect us from it. Or to say it positively, God delights in protecting us from temptation, so let's ask him to do it. Some of Satan's plots to tempt us will surely be foiled because God answers our prayers.

Choose God's Presence

While calling out for God's help, we must also choose his presence.[8] After all, holiness requires fleeing both from sin and to God. We "flee youthful passions" (2 Tim. 2:22). But we must always unite abstaining from sin with heeding the equally important command to delight in God. By faith, we choose him, his pleasure, his reward, and his fellowship over the promise of sin. This decision is conscious and intentional and requires sober-mindedness.

Years ago, I was scrolling on social media and saw a seductive image. I had a decision to make in that moment. My flesh cried out with hungry curiosity, "Oh! What was that? You should scroll back and look!" At the same time, a promise from Jesus that I'd stored in my heart cried out, "Blessed are the pure in heart, for they shall see God" (Matt. 5:8).

I had a decision to make. By God's grace, I prayed aloud, "Lord, help me to resist sin so I can see you and know you more!" I then blocked the post, deleted the app, and sent a text to my wife and a friend saying, "I just saw a seductive image online. I didn't click or linger on it, but I resisted the temptation. I just wanted you to know so you could pray for me."

That day I chose the presence of God rather than the pleasure of sin. Thousands of days later, I'm still thankful. You'll never regret resisting sin; you'll always regret giving in.

Consume God's Grace

Fighting sin and temptation also involves consuming God's grace. After all, "You are what you eat." This adage proves true not only for our physical health but also for the health of our souls (Gal. 6:7–8). What happens if you fill your spare moments soaking in sports or shows or social media, or daydreaming about an alternative life? Your affections for God will become weak and half-hearted.

But if you consume truths about God and the gospel, you will cultivate heavenly affections. Strong affections for God fuels obedience to God. Jesus promised, "Blessed are those who hunger and thirst for righteousness, for they shall be satisfied" (Matt. 5:6). God calls us to feast and be satisfied in him rather than settle for sin.[9]

1. Scripture: Feast on God's Word

Listening to God produces love for God.[10] We need to regularly step away from the many responsibilities and distractions of our lives to hear God's voice by reading the Bible. Jesus assures us, "Man shall not live by bread alone, but by every word that comes from the mouth of God" (Matt. 4:4). As bodies cannot survive without food, so our souls will starve if we neglect God's word. Feast on God's word, and store it up in your heart that you might not sin against him (Ps. 119:11).

Feasting on Scripture brings you face-to-face with the author of Scripture, God himself, and provides power for the fight against sin. Open your Bible and allow his holiness to humble you, his wisdom comfort you, his beauty captivate you, and his love astound you. Consume God's word personally each day, but also commit to being part of a local church where you can hear God's word proclaimed faithfully each week. Don't underestimate how important hearing faithful sermons is to your battle with sin.

In my time as a pastor I've repeatedly witnessed the role that faithful, Bible-soaked sermons play in helping saints fight against their sin. Consider this sister's testimony about how the preaching of God's word in her local church has helped her over the years:

> It's sermons like the one you preached yesterday that had such a shaping effect on me in the first few years. . . . You know about the struggles I had with anxiety and depression, and a major reason why I am free of that today is due to the gospel-saturated teaching I received and the way the gospel was applied as I lived life within our church community. Ultimately, it is a miracle of

God to free me from the grip fear and despair had on me, but he used our church's teaching and community to help show me the path to freedom through the gospel.

God uses his word proclaimed from the pulpit, portrayed in the ordinances, and applied in the church community to help us be strengthened to resist sin and follow him.[11]

2. Prayer and Fasting: Delight in God[12]

Do you pray? We live in an age of abounding distraction. Regular time of unhurried, honest prayer is scarce. But if you will find any help in fighting temptation to sin, you must pray. We require strength to wage spiritual war, so endure in prayer (Eph. 6:10–18). Retreat from everyday duties to speak with God (Matt. 6:6). Just as you breathe continually, pray continually (1 Thess. 5:17). Apart from Christ we can do nothing, so plead for him to help you (John 15:5).[13]

Do you fast? Faith-filled fasting is one of the most potent weapons in warring against sin. Sin is about self-indulgence and satisfying the flesh.

Fasting starves out our sinful urges. When we fast, we say no to something in order to say yes to focused time with God. By telling our body no to something it's craving (food, entertainment, etc.), we're reawakened to the fact that we're dependent creatures. And this gives us opportunity to cry out, "As my body hungers for food, make my soul hunger for you."

Like all disciplines, mere prayer and fasting will not fill you with the joy of Jesus. In fact, God often uses them to expose our grumpiness about our discomfort. But when we prayerfully fast in faith, God starves our sin and focuses our sight on him.

3. Music: Stir Your Soul with Singing

Tune-wrapped truths have a way of informing our minds and warming our souls up to God. Music reaches through the ear and elevates our weary hearts to behold the one who stands ready to help. Make a playlist of songs you can turn on when you're feeling tempted. Temptation disorients, but uplifting lyrics can drown out sin's voice and point your soul to its only satisfaction.

When Saul was afflicted by a demon, David ministered to him through music, and his anxiety abated (1 Sam. 16:14–23).[14] When lust or discontentment or jealousy usher you toward dark fantasies, turn up songs that remind you of the beauty, sufficiency, and glory of Christ. Allow yourself to be ministered to by Jesus-glorifying music, and plead with God to help you believe his truth rather than the tempter's lies.

4. Creation: Be Amazed by His Wisdom

Nature may be one of God's most surprising weapons against sin. Beholding God's beauty in creation captivates our hearts in a way that produces thankfulness. Whether a walk outside during a work break, a drive through the country or by the coastline, or pausing to gaze at the stars while taking out the trash at night—considering God's handiwork in creation humbles us and reacquaints us with God's worthiness (Pss. 19:1–6; 104:1–35). Depression and doubt can be muffled by the sound of a rushing river. The singing of birds can remind us to cast our anxieties on God who cares for us. The smell of honeysuckle or the brilliance of a sunset can remind our prideful hearts that God's ways are wiser than ours. Regularly retreat to creation and ask God to help you see how his handiwork is better than whatever sin offers you.

Before moving on to the next point, I want to remind you that each of these practices isn't a magic formula that will automatically help you fight sin. Reading Scripture, praying, listening to God-centered music, and beholding God's glory in creation are simply avenues to help us see the glory of Christ and trust more firmly in the promises of the gospel. Only by beholding Jesus are we spiritually transformed (2 Cor. 3:18).

Martyn Lloyd-Jones, one of the greatest preachers of the twentieth century, explained this point masterfully:

A friend was asking me the other day, "How can I be humble?" He felt there was pride in him, and he wanted to know how to get rid of it. He seemed to think that

I had some patent remedy and could tell him, "Do this, that, and the other and you will be humble." I said, "I have no method or technique. I can't tell you to get down on your knees and believe in prayer because I know you will soon be proud of that. There's only one way to be humble, and that is to look into the face of Jesus Christ; you cannot be anything else when you see him." That is the only way. Humility is not something you can create within yourself; rather, you look at him, you realize who he is and what he has done, and you are humbled.[15]

Lloyd-Jones isn't dismissing the importance of effort. He's reminding us that true change comes only from beholding Jesus. Read to see Jesus. Pray to draw near to Jesus. Fast to hunger for more of Jesus. Sing to shape your affections around Jesus. Behold creation to cultivate adoration of Jesus. Nurture nearness to Jesus, and you'll be conformed to his likeness.

Cultivate Holy Community

The fight against sin and temptation also requires cultivating holy community.

Jacqueline's fear of man tempted her toward deceitfulness. Her conversations were marked by "little" lies, partial truths, and exaggerations. She masked her sin and intentionally left out information that led to creating a world where she was deeply isolated despite often being around people. No one really knew her, and it crippled her walk with God.

Are you opening your life to trusted Christian friends in an honest way? Are you developing intentionally intrusive relationships in which you are giving and receiving godly encouragement, confession, and rebuke?

We are too weak to make it to heaven by ourselves. Hear afresh this warning:

Take care, brothers [and sisters], lest there be in any of you an evil, unbelieving heart, leading you to fall away from the living God. But exhort one another every day, as long as it is called "today," that none of

you may be hardened by the deceitfulness
of sin. (Heb. 3:12–13)

God's antidote for spiritual atrophy and apostasy
is gospel community. This is why committing
to a local church and growing in honest community is not optional for the believer.

Jacqueline's life changed when she finally
allowed a friend to know the "real her." It took a
while for her to learn to speak the truth, but God
used that friend to help her take actual steps
toward freedom from sin.

Create Intentional Defenses

To fight sin we must also create intentional de-
fenses. How would you respond if you learned
that a lion had escaped from the local zoo and
was spotted in your neighborhood? You'd be on
high alert. You'd shut gates and lock doors. Why?
Because a lion will devour you.

God warns us a lion *is* on the loose: "Be
sober-minded; be watchful. Your adversary the
devil prowls around like a roaring lion, seeking
someone to devour" (1 Pet. 5:8).

To avoid the prowling tempter, you must set up intentional protection against temptation. You must "make no provision for the flesh" (Rom. 13:14) by setting up barbwire, as it were, at all access points. Make it as difficult as possible for you to access something that is sin or might lead you to sin.

For instance, my family has smartphones, computers, gaming systems, and a smart TV. To guard us against seductive content, I currently have *six different layers* of technological protection.[16] Why? Because the world is designed to make holiness hard and sinning easy. So if we're going to have internet in our home, I must ensure our guard is up.

How do sin and temptation make their way into your heart and life? Do certain shows or social media apps provoke discontentment or envy? What keeps you from eliminating them? Do you access sinful content on your phone or other devices? Are you taking steps to limit your freedom by having a friend install restrictions on your devices?

You may be hesitant to limit your freedoms, but remember Jesus's sobering words:

If your right eye causes you to sin, tear it out and throw it away. For it is better that you lose one of your members than that your whole body be thrown into hell. And if your right hand causes you to sin, cut it off and throw it away. For it is better that you lose one of your members than that your whole body go into hell. (Matt. 5:29–30)

Jesus is saying that we must be willing to do whatever it takes to keep from giving in to sin and temptation.

Consider Sin's Consequences

Sin always hides the price tag, which is why fighting it also requires us to consider sin's consequences. Temptation is presented in a way that covers what it will cost if you give in to it. A helpful way to fight sin's deception is to envision its end; consider where it will lead if you follow.[17]

Scripture warns us, "The tongue is a fire, a world of unrighteousness . . . , setting on fire the entire course of life, and set on fire by hell"

(James 3:6). Consider the destructive nature of gossip and slander. When secrets are shared or rumors are spread, they have devastating effects. Skepticism is stoked. Trust is broken. Love is cooled. Families are fractured. Churches are split. Lives are altered. Decade-long friendships are ruptured because details shared in confidence were spread carelessly.

Remember that your sin never affects just you. It always affects others. Sin promises it will be worth it, but it never is. Consider sin's consequences and resist its offerings.

Confess Sinful Compromise[18]

Finally, fighting sin and temptation requires us to confess sinful compromise.

Admittedly, telling others about our sin is scary. None of us like to have our shameful deeds displayed before others. Just like Adam and Eve after they sinned in the garden of Eden, we cover our compromising lives and hide in the shadows of deceit (Gen. 3:7–8). Sin tells us that we're safe behind the mask of lies, but we're not. In the dark shadows, we change. We tell lies and eventually believe them. We resist the Spirit's nudges and quench his convicting voice. Slowly, living with hidden lies becomes normal.

Confessing sin to God and another believer rips off the mask of hypocrisy so we can breathe the air of honesty. It enlivens our heart to feel again, and it removes the veil so we can see Christ afresh. Confession humbles us, which by nature uproots the pride that keeps immorality alive and attractive to our souls.

Let's break down this last point into several steps.

1. Ask God to Convict You of Sin

Conviction is an act of mercy that awakens us to our guilt before a holy God. His Spirit graciously makes us aware of ways we have sinned against him. Ask him to show you your sin; pray with a surrendered heart,

> Search me, O God, and know my heart!
> Try me and know my thoughts!

And see if there be any grievous way
>   in me,
>   and lead me in the way everlasting!
>   (Ps. 139:23–24)

2. Confess Your Sin to God

God doesn't just want us to be aware of the fact that we're sinners; he wants us to acknowledge it to him. Confession means agreeing with God that we've sinned and done what is evil in his sight. Proverbs 28:13 assures us, "Whoever conceals his transgressions will not prosper, but he who confesses and forsakes them will obtain mercy." God loves to give mercy, so confess your sins to him, knowing that "if we confess our sins, he is faithful and just to forgive us our sins and to cleanse us from all unrighteousness" (1 John 1:9). Speak honestly to God, and tell him what you have done.[19]

3. Confess Your Sin to Others[20]

James 5:16 says clearly, "Confess your sins to one another and pray for one another, that you may be healed." God assures us that while our relationship with him is personal, it's not private. Because we're a body, what we do in our personal lives affects our brothers and sisters in Christ. How can we speak the truth to one another "in love" (Eph. 4:15) and "not lie to one another" (Col. 3:9) if we don't speak honestly about our sins.

Who knows your intimate temptations and sins? If no one in your life knows your weaknesses, temptations, and sin patterns, then you are in danger. Ask God to give you courage to speak with another trusted believer about your pursuit of holiness. Here are some specific steps you can take:

> *Confess to a small group of friends.* It is unwise and unnecessary for everyone to know everything about you. But someone should know. Find mature, trusted friends and share your struggles.

> *Share your temptations.* Temptation is not sin, but it is dangerous. Secrecy strengthens sin; light saps it. I have often found that temptation flees when I tell a friend that I'm facing it.

Confess sin quickly. The longer you wait
to confess, the more likely you won't
confess it. Sin is a cancer, so root it out
quickly.

Confess sin honestly. The temptation to lie
about what we've done is very strong.
You don't want to share too many details to lead someone else into sin, but
you ought to share enough to give a full
picture of how you've compromised.

Who knows you? *Really* knows you? Who
has permission to ask you penetrating questions *and* is also acting on that permission?
Furthermore, are you being honest with that
person? Are you answering questions evasively
or trying to project an image of someone you're
not? Knowing the freedom of Christ comes by
traveling the path of honesty. God will help you.
Step into the light.

Chase True Freedom

The most glorious truth of the gospel is that
through the death and resurrection of Jesus,

we can be forgiven of our sins. We don't have to spend an eternity in hell under God's wrath. But did you know the gospel promises us even more than that? Jesus rose from the dead to liberate you from sin's enslaving power, starting the day you believe! "The Lord Jesus . . . gave himself for our sins to deliver us from the present evil age" (Gal. 1:3–4; cf. John 8:36). In Christ we can know real, true freedom from sin. Peter therefore exhorts us, "Live as people who are free" (1 Pet. 2:16).

Child of God, do not forget that you don't have to do what you used to do because you aren't who you used to be (Rom. 6:1–14). You have been united to Christ and raised to live a new life of freedom. To walk in freedom, we must understand what freedom is and what it isn't.

Freedom Isn't Sinlessness

While we certainly strive not to sin and trust that God always gives a way of escape (1 Cor. 10:13), we also need to remember that no one reaches sinless perfection in this life. The apostle Paul said, "Not that I have already obtained this [the resurrection] or am already perfect, but I press on to make it my own, because Christ Jesus has made me his own" (Phil. 3:12). We have not arrived, but we aim our hearts toward that day when we will be perfect with Christ (1 John 3:1–3). While we long to be made perfect, our walk with Jesus is much more about direction than perfection in this life.

Freedom Isn't Superficial

God does not merely call us to behavior modification. He desires heart transformation. Jesus said, "Blessed are the pure in heart, for they shall see God" (Matt. 5:8). This means purity is not an end in itself but rather a means to the end of knowing God. So, yes, stop looking at pornography, stop stealing, stop speaking deceitfully, stop giving in to sinful anger. But the reason we do so is so that we can see, know, and please God.

Freedom Isn't Instantaneous

God does not change us quickly or all at once. Sanctification is more like cooking with a crockpot than a microwave. It is by our continually looking to Jesus that God continually changes us from "one degree of glory to another" (2 Cor. 3:18). This change, however, often happens at a painfully slow pace. It is often a moment-by-moment, day-by-day, week-by-week struggle, but God has promised to complete the work and make us like Jesus (Phil. 1:6). Remembering this helps us have persevering patience with ourselves and those we minister to.

Freedom Is Spirit Filled

True freedom is Spirit-filled freedom: "You were called to freedom, brothers." So "walk by the Spirit, and you will not gratify the desires of the flesh" (Gal. 5:13, 16). The Holy Spirit unites us with Jesus and manifests his life in us (Rom. 8:9–11, 29). This is true freedom. Sin corrupts our humanity by enslaving us to sinful passions, but the Spirit frees us to be like Jesus. We are never more alive than when we are like Christ.

May God's Spirit grant you enduring freedom by exposing sin, encouraging growth, and pointing you to the ever-abounding mercy of Christ.

What If I Fail?

As a young believer, I often rode a spiritual roller coaster. I'd go from being full of joyful zeal for Christ to compromising with sin and falling into crippling guilt. After sinning, I would fast and make vows to God, only to fall again. Years of this enslaving pattern finally ended when a friend taught me a liberating truth: the gospel is for believers, too.

The good news of God's grace isn't only for sinners barreling toward hell; it is also for saints struggling toward heaven. When we come to Christ, we don't stop being weak, desperate, sinful people in need of grace. In fact, we become more aware of our need for grace! Thankfully, God supplies what we need.

The apostle John penned these words for struggling saints: "My little children, I am writing these things to you so that you may not sin. But if anyone does sin, we have an advocate with the Father, Jesus Christ the righteous" (1 John 2:1). John effectively says, "I hope you don't sin anymore, but if you do, there is somewhere to turn—to Jesus!"

Sin calls you to look in, but God calls you to look up to Christ. He stands as our ever-living, ever-interceding high priest (Heb. 4:14–16). If you fail, cast yourself on Jesus. Go to him quickly so that sin will have no opportunity to deepen its roots. Go to him boldly, knowing that he shed his blood for you and rose for you. Confess your sin honestly to him, trusting that he loves you despite your failure. Cling to his promise of forgiveness. Commit to repent in whatever way necessary. Call a community of friends to help you. No believer makes it home free from sin, but Christ can keep you from stumbling (Jude 24–25).

When Sin Shall Be No More

We will not battle evil forever. Soon, the Lord Jesus will return and take us to a land where sin and temptation shall be only distant memories. In that land God's purposes will be fulfilled and God's people will, as the old hymn says, "be saved to sin no more."[21]

When Christ returns, a radical transformation will take place. In that moment, we shall be made like him (1 John 3:2–3). All evil desires will be eradicated and replaced with ever-increasing enjoyment of God. Whispers of temptation will forever be silenced and give way to the sound of God singing over us with joy (Zeph. 3:17).

When we set our hope on that day, we are empowered for obedience in this day. The more we long to see him and be with him, the less appealing sin and temptation will be. Keep the eyes of your heart on Christ, lock arms with fellow believers, and press on in holiness. Do not grow weary. We're almost home.

Recommended Resources

Jerry Bridges, *The Pursuit of Holiness* (Colorado Springs: NavPress, 2006).

Jerry Bridges, *Respectable Sins: Confronting the Sins we Tolerate* (Colorado Springs: NavPress, 2007).

Thomas Brooks, *Precious Remedies against Satan's Devices* (1652; repr., Carlisle, PA: Banner of Truth, 2021).

J. Garrett Kell, *Pure in Heart: Sexual Sin and the Promises of God* (Wheaton, IL: Crossway, 2021).

John Piper, *Future Grace: The Purifying Power of the Promises of God* (Colorado Springs: Multnomah, 2012).

J. C. Ryle, *Holiness* (1877; repr., Carlisle, PA: Banner of Truth, 2014).

Notes

1. *The New City Catechism: 52 Questions and Answers for Our Hearts and Minds* (Wheaton, IL: Crossway), q. 16 (46–47). Cf. Westminster Shorter Catechism q. 14; Westminster Larger Catechism q. 24; and Benjamin Keach's Catechism q. 18, in *The Philadelphia Confession of Faith Being the London Confession of Faith Adopted by the Baptist Association 1742, with Scripture References and Keach's Catechism* (Sterling, VA: Grace Abounding Ministries, 1977).

2. Shai Linne, "Atonement Q&A," on *The Atonement* (Lamp Mode, 2008).

3. For the believer, this death refers primarily to missing the abundant life of Spirit-filled peace and joy that comes in fellowship with God. It can also, however, refer to physical sickness or death that God may ordain as an act of discipline for unrepentant sin (1 Cor. 11:30).

4. This does not deny the fact that sinful desires are sin. For instance, feeling sexual attraction toward a

member of the same sex is evidence of our fallen nature. If one resists giving in to unnatural desires, they are not sinning and do not need to feel perpetually displeasing to God.

5. C. S. Lewis, *The Weight of Glory* (1941; repr., New York, NY: HarperCollins 1980), 26.

6. Inspired by John Owen, *Mortification of Sin* (1656; repr., Carlisle PA: Banner of Truth, 2022), chap. 5; and Thomas Chalmers, *The Expulsive Power of a New Affection* (Wheaton, IL: Crossway, 2020).

7. "Deliver us from the evil one" is a reasonable translation that would be a plea to protect us from Satan.

8. Some content in this paragraph is adapted from J. Garrett Kell, *Pure in Heart: Sexual Sin and the Promises of God* (Wheaton, IL: Crossway, 2021), 28.

9. For a more in-depth discussion, see Kell, *Pure in Heart*, chap. 6.

10. Content in this section has been reproduced from J. Garrett Kell, "Draw Near to the Lord in Your Fight for Purity," Crossway.org, November 1, 2021, https://www.crossway.org/.

11. Baptism and the Lord's Supper provide fresh reminders of God's saving and sustaining mercies. As we partake of them in faith, the Spirit strengthens our communion with Jesus and deepens our love for other believers.

12. You might think, *Didn't we just talk about prayer?* Yes, but I'm betting you could use another reminder. Content in this section is adapted from Kell, "Draw Near to the Lord in Your Fight for Purity."

13. I highly commend *A Call to Prayer* by J. C. Ryle to aid your prayer life.

14. Sure, Saul did wig out a couple of times and threw a spear at David's head (1 Sam. 18:10–11), but the ministry of music clearly had some soothing effect on Saul's soul.

15. Martyn Lloyd-Jones, *Living Water: Studies in John 4* (Wheaton, IL: Crossway, 2009), 710.

16. These include parental controls, Domain Name System (DNS) filtering, program filters, passwords, and reporting software.

17. To see this applied to sexual temptation, consider Garrett Kell, "Envision the End of Your Sin," The Gospel Coalition, August 7, 2017, https://www.thegospel coalition.org/.

18. Some content in this section is adapted from Kell, *Pure in Heart*, 119–20.

19. To aid your prayer, consider using Psalm 51 as a model. It is a confession by David of his sin against God. Other useful Scriptures to aid your confession are Pss. 32; 38; 103; 130; and 1 John 1:5–10.

20. Content in this section is adapted from Kell, *Pure in Heart*, 120–22.

21. William Cowper, "There Is a Fountain Filled with Blood," in *Conyers's Collection of Psalms and Hymns* (London: Clement Watts, 1772).

Scripture Index

IX 9Marks

Building Healthy Churches

9Marks exists to equip church leaders with a biblical vision and practical resources for displaying God's glory to the nations through healthy churches.

To that end, we want to see churches characterized by these nine marks of health:

1. Expositional Preaching
2. Gospel Doctrine
3. A Biblical Understanding of Conversion and Evangelism
4. Biblical Church Membership
5. Biblical Church Discipline
6. A Biblical Concern for Discipleship and Growth
7. Biblical Church Leadership
8. A Biblical Understanding of the Practice of Prayer
9. A Biblical Understanding and Practice of Missions

Find all our Crossway titles and other resources at 9Marks.org.